MAKING **HISTORY**

ANCIENT
ROME

Fiona Macdonald and Sue Nicholson

W

FRANKLIN WATTS
LONDON • SYDNEY

First published in 2008 by Franklin Watts

Copyright © Franklin Watts 2008

Franklin Watts
338 Euston Road
London NW1 3BH

Franklin Watts Australia
Level 17/207 Kent Street
Sydney, NSW 2000

A CIP catalogue record for this book is available
from the British Library.

Created by Q2AMedia
Editor: Jean Coppendale
Creative Director: Simmi Sikka
Sr. Art Director: Ashita Murgai
Sr. Designers: Dibakar Acharjee
Senior Project Manager: Kavita Lad
Project Manager: Gaurav Seth
Picture Researcher: Amit Tigga, Jyoti Sachdeva
Art, Craft & Photography: Tarang Saggar
Illustrators: Amit Tayal, Rajesh Das
Models: Radhika Bharti, Daniel Willis, Ruchi Sharma (Hands)

Dewey number: 937

ISBN 978 0 7496 7849 4

Note to parents and teachers:
Every effort has been made by the Publisher to ensure that the websites in this book are suitable for children, that they
are of the highest educational value, and that they contain no inappropriate or offensive material. However, because of the nature
of the Internet, it is impossible to guarantee that the contents of these sites will not be altered. We strongly advise that Internet
access is supervised by a responsible adult.

Many projects in this book require adult supervision, especially those which involve the use
of scissors and craft knives. Some projects suggest the use of wallpaper paste. It is advised that a fungicide-free
paste (cellulose paste) is used. If in doubt, consult the manufacturer's contents list and instructions. Many projects suggest
the use of paint. It is advised that non-toxic paint is used. If in doubt, consult the manufacturer's contents list and instructions.

Picture Credits:
Cover: Q2AMedia
t: top, b: bottom, m: middle, c: centre, l: left, r: right
p4: Imagestate /Photolibrary (top left); p4: Clara Natoli/ Shutterstock (bottom); p6: Danilo Ascione / Shutterstock (top right);
p6: Vanni Archive/CORBIS (bottom); p7:Lebrecht Music and Arts Photo Library / Alamy (Top); p10 Vittoriano Rastelli/CORBIS (bottom);
p11: SIMON FRASER / Photolibrary (top right); p12: wyrdlight / Alamy (botom); p14: Ulrike Hammerich / Shutterstock (top left);
p14:TERRY SHEILA / Photolibrary (bottom); p16 Clara Natoli / Shutterstock (bottom); p18:THE BRIDGEMAN ART LIBRARY / Photolibrary
(top right); p18: Imagestate /Photolibrary (bottom);p19: Lebrecht Music and Arts Photo Library / Alamy ;p22: The Art Archive/Corbis(bottom);
p24:Visual Arts Library (London) / Alamy (bottom); p26:Vittoriano Rastelli/CORBIS (left); p26:The Art Archive/Corbis (bottom);
p28: INTERFOTO Pressebildagentur / Alamy (bottom)

Printed in China

Franklin Watts is a division of Hachette Children's Books, an Hachette Livre UK company.

www.hachettelivre.co.uk

Contents

What do we know about the Romans?

The Romans lived in Italy around 2,000 years ago. They ruled one of the largest and richest empires the world has ever seen.

▲ Some Romans displayed their portraits on pieces of wood attached to their coffins. These are a record of what Romans wore and how they looked.

▼ Many great Roman buildings are now in ruins, such as this forum at Leptis Magna, Tunisia. The style and size of the ruins give us clues about the power and glory of the Roman Empire.

A lasting influence

Roman power lasted for centuries, from around 350 BC to almost AD 400. But then Roman lands were attacked by invaders from the east and north. In AD 476, the last Roman emperor was forced to leave Rome.

Today, we still use Roman words, including 'animal' and 'victory', and write using the Roman alphabet. Some of us have Roman names, such as Anthony, Honor or Rufus. We still enjoy Roman stories, myths and legends, and Roman entertainments, especially gladiator fights, have inspired many computer games and films.

SCOTLAND

North Sea

IRELAND

Hadrian's Wall

Roman bath

BRITAIN

London

Cologne

GERMANY

Atlantic Ocean

Paris

Amphitheatre

FRANCE

Aqueduct

Temple

SPAIN

Cadiz

CORSICA

Colosseum

ITALY

Rome

SARDINIA

Black Sea

Constantinople

TURKEY

MIDDLE
EAST

Walls around new Roman
capital, Constantinople,
started AD 324

Caspian Sea

SYRIA

Babylon

GREECE

Carthage

SICILY

Athens

CRETE

Mediterranean Sea

CYPRUS

Jerusalem

AFRICA

Alexandria

EGYPT

Key

■ Roman Empire, AD 117

The Roman Empire at its greatest extent. ▲

How do we know?

Many different sorts of evidence have survived
to tell us about Roman times.

Magnificent buildings We can still see
the ruins of Roman monuments, temples and
arenas. We can visit splendid Roman buildings
and structures, such as the Hadrian's Wall.

Archaeological treasures Archaeologists
have discovered many remains of Roman life.
These include houses, weapons, pottery, coins,
metalwork, glass and even human and
animal bones.

Art and craftwork Paintings, statues,
carvings and mosaics made by Roman artists
and craft workers are displayed in museums and
heritage centres for us to study and admire.

Written records Roman poets, scholars and
historians wrote down many descriptions of
Roman life, which we can still read today.

City and people

The city of Rome was built on seven hills beside the River Tiber. According to legend, it was founded in 753 BC. It grew fast, and became the heart of the mighty Roman Empire. By AD 300, it was home to over a million people.

Roman government

Most Romans were plebeians – ordinary working men, women and children. There were also many slaves. Until 509 BC, Romans were ruled by kings, but then the city became a republic. Every year, the senate, a committee of rich, respected patricians (nobles), elected two consuls (judges) to lead the government. In 27 BC, Augustus, Rome's most powerful general, seized power after a civil war. He became Rome's first emperor. Rome was then ruled by emperors, until Roman power collapsed in AD 476.

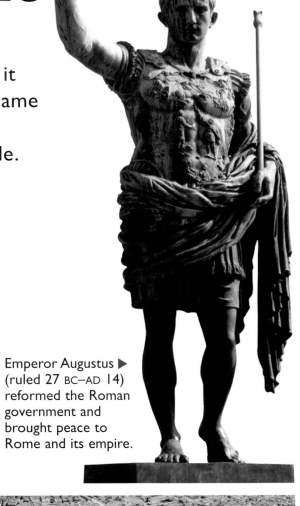

Emperor Augustus ▶ (ruled 27 BC–AD 14) reformed the Roman government and brought peace to Rome and its empire.

The River Tiber

The Circus Maximus (oval horse-race track)

The Colosseum

Emperor Claudius's Temple

This model shows ▶ the city of Rome around AD 300.

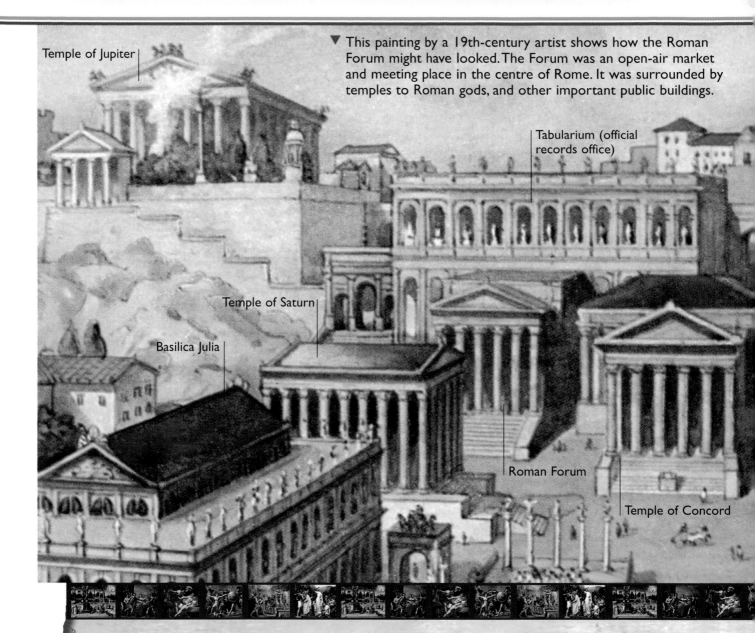

Temple of Jupiter

This painting by a 19th-century artist shows how the Roman Forum might have looked. The Forum was an open-air market and meeting place in the centre of Rome. It was surrounded by temples to Roman gods, and other important public buildings.

Tabularium (official records office)

Temple of Saturn

Basilica Julia

Roman Forum

Temple of Concord

Roman rulers

Romulus (ruled c. 753 BC) Legendary first king. Said to be the son of the war-god Mars, and raised by a wolf.

Tarquin the Proud (ruled 534–510 BC) Last king of Rome. Hated as a tyrant and murderer. Was overthrown.

Julius Caesar (lived 100–44 BC) Brave, tough, popular army commander. Conquered Gaul (France), invaded Britain. Killed by fellow senators who thought he had too much power.

Augustus (ruled 27 BC–AD 14) A great army leader and nephew of Julius Caesar. Defeated his rivals Mark Antony and Queen Cleopatra of Egypt. First ruler of the Roman Empire.

Nero (ruled AD 54–68) Artistic, musical, extravagant, cruel. Unfairly blamed Christians for starting the Great Fire in Rome (AD 64), and then persecuted them.

Hadrian (ruled AD 117–138) Born in Spain. Tried to bring peace. Built a massive wall to defend England from Scotland.

Constantine the Great (ruled AD 312–337) Built Constantinople (now Istanbul, Turkey) as a new capital for the Empire. Gave religious freedom to all the Empire's inhabitants.

Dress like a Roman

The Ancient Romans wore clothes made of wool or linen. Men wore a toga or a simple tunic. Women wore a long dress called a stola, which was fastened with brooches, and a palla, or shawl. This project shows you how to make a tunic and a brooch, so you can dress like an Ancient Roman.

You can make a girl's ▶ stola in the same way as the boy's tunic – simply use a longer piece of fabric that will reach your ankles when folded.

Glue blue or gold braid around the neck of the tunic

Turn to page 24 to find out how to make a bulla – a pouch containing a lucky charm

Wear the palla draped across your shoulder

Boy's tunic

1

Ask an adult to cut out a piece of cloth measuring 60cm x 200–220cm (using pinking shears, so the fabric won't fray). Fold the fabric in half lengthways, then cut a curved slit for the neck hole.

Roman brooch

1

Cut out some circles of card. Make patterns on the circles with glue.

2

Glue the long edges together at each side with fabric glue, leaving space for the armholes. When the glue is dry, turn the tunic the right side out.

3

Tie the tunic at your waist with a piece of cord.

You will need

For the tunic:
- Fabric, such as a large sheet
- Tape measure
- Pinking shears • Fabric glue
- Cord or ribbon

For the tunic:
- Cardboard • Scissors
- Plastic jewels • PVA glue
- Safety pin • Sticky tape
- Silver or gold foil

2

When the glue is dry, cover the brooch with silver or gold foil and stick on some plastic jewels.

3

Fix a safety pin on the back of each brooch with sticky tape or a blob of glue.

Army and empire

The Roman army was one of the most successful armies in history. Soldiers were well-trained, well-led and well-paid, and they were equipped with excellent armour and weapons. Thousands of men volunteered to join the army.

▼ Roman armies marched into battle in close formation. Each man was armed with a sword, a dagger and two spears.

Army standard was always carried into battle

Strong, flexible armour made of metal strips; worn over a red woollen tunic

Centurion (senior officer) shouting orders

Wooden shields have a curved metal boss (cover) in the centre to protect the soldier's hand

Testudo (tortoise) battle formation. The soldiers interlock their shields to protect themselves against flying spears

Stone carving showing ▼ Romans (top of picture) defending their fort against attacking enemy tribes around AD 110.

A magnificent empire

From around 330 BC, armies from Rome began to conquer land. By AD 117, when Roman power reached its peak, Rome ruled an empire stretching from Scotland and Germany to Egypt and Syria. Everyone living in the empire had to pay Roman taxes and obey Roman laws. The conquered peoples used Roman coins and were governed by Roman officials. Some learned to speak Latin, the Romans' language, as well.

Celtic chiefs rode into battle on fast chariots pulled by horses

Celtic warrior wears blue body paint and carries a decorated shield

Celts attack with spears hurled towards the Romans

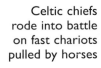
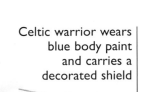

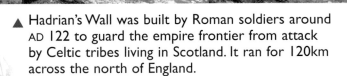

▲ Hadrian's Wall was built by Roman soldiers around AD 122 to guard the empire frontier from attack by Celtic tribes living in Scotland. It ran for 120km across the north of England.

Copying the conquered

Everywhere they ruled, the Romans introduced their own way of life. They built cities, temples, villas and sports arenas. But they also learned from the peoples they conquered. For example, the Romans adopted many different gods from the countries in their empire, as well as styles of architecture. They also took their alphabet from Greece. Roman soldiers even copied British warriors by wearing trousers under their tunics to keep warm.

Rebels against Rome

People in the countries conquered by the Romans often fought back. Here are just three examples.

Gauls (France): <u>War-hero Vercingetorix</u>: Rebelled against Julius Caesar's army in 52 BC. Vercingetorix was captured, paraded through the streets of Rome, then executed in 46 BC.

British: <u>Queen Boudicca of Iceni tribe</u>: Led a revenge attack on Romans. Destroyed Roman cities, including London, AD 60–61. Defeated in battle. She took poison to avoid capture.

Jews: <u>Zealots</u> (Jewish patriots): Occupied Masada fort, near the Dead Sea, and defended it against the Roman army, AD 66–73. They committed suicide rather than surrender.

Make a Roman standard

Each legion (a troop of about 5,000 soldiers) in the Roman army had its own standard, which was carried into every battle. The standard was a tall pole decorated with symbols, such as animals and laurel wreaths, which represented the unit's successes in battle. The most important standard was the eagle, which was carried by a special standard bearer. If a legion lost its eagle to an enemy, the legion faced great dishonour and was disbanded.

Into battle

Standards were tall so that soldiers could see them in battle. This made it easier for units to stay together when fighting. It also encouraged soldiers to be brave and fight well for the honour and glory of Rome.

▲ Today, troops of men interested in Roman history research weapons and armour, and re-enact Roman battles. This helps us understand what Roman warfare was really like.

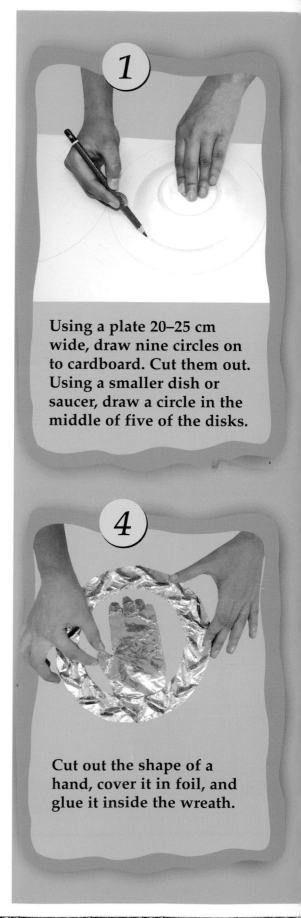

1

Using a plate 20–25 cm wide, draw nine circles on to cardboard. Cut them out. Using a smaller dish or saucer, draw a circle in the middle of five of the disks.

4

Cut out the shape of a hand, cover it in foil, and glue it inside the wreath.

2

Ask an adult to help you cut out the centres of five of the circles to make frames. Glue four of the frames on to the remaining four circles and cover them with foil.

You will need

- Thick cardboard
- Plate and saucer
- Wooden broom handle
- Metallic paint • Paintbrush
- Scissors • Pencil
- PVA glue • Silver foil
- Red ribbon • Strong tape

3

Make the fifth round frame into a laurel wreath by drawing a pattern of leaves on to the card with thick glue. When dry, cover the wreath in silver foil.

The famous Roman letters SPQR stand for *senatus populusque Romanus*, which means 'the senate and people of Rome'. The letters appear on coins and inscriptions, as well as on army standards.

6

Glue two small foil-covered circles on to red ribbons and glue them to the back of the card. Tape all the shapes to a broom handle as shown right.

5

Cut out a rectangle of card and the letters S, P, Q and R (ask an adult to help). Cover the card in foil and paint the letters in metallic paint. Glue the letters on to the card.

Brilliant builders

The Romans were great inventors. They made many things that were useful for people living in towns and cities, and for Roman soldiers. Many top Roman designers, doctors, architects and engineers worked for the army.

▲ The Pont du Gard, a Roman aqueduct in the South of France. The channel carrying fresh drinking water from the mountains to the city is supported across a valley on rows of arches, a Roman invention.

Building the best

Romans were the first to design and build aqueducts, water pipes, underground drains and public lavatories. They pioneered the use of concrete (made with ash from Italian volcanoes), and built 85,000km of straight roads across their empire, so that soldiers could march quickly to any trouble spot.

Roman homes were also carefully designed. Rich people paid for elegant town houses, planned to provide privacy and security. These had high, windowless outer walls and cool, inner courtyard gardens. Poor people lived in wooden shacks or tall blocks designed to house as many people as possible.

Many streets in Roman cities were lined ▶ with insulae (apartment blocks). These were often badly built and landlords charged high rents but did not look after them.

▲ This mosaic shows a Roman country villa in Tunisia, North Africa.

Raised pavement for pedestrians

Walls are made of bricks, wood and plaster. Roofs are covered with tiles of baked clay

Horses and donkeys carry heavy loads

Families live in rented rooms above shops

Slave shouts to bring customers to his master's shop

Food shops and taverns sell bread, sausages, snacks and wine

Public baths

The Romans knew that keeping clean and taking exercise were good ways to stay healthy. They built public bathhouses for everyone to use in towns and cities.

Entry to a bathhouse was very cheap, or free. There were separate bath times for men and women. Inside, bathhouses had steam rooms, where bathers' sweat helped loosen the dirt on their skin. Then slaves rubbed bathers with warm olive oil and scraped it off, together with any dirt and sweat that remained.

Once they were clean, bathers had a choice of warm, hot or cold pools for swimming or just relaxing. Some bathhouses had hairdressers and rooms for beauty treatments, massages and sports, as well as snack bars, libraries and art galleries. Many rich people had private bathhouses in their own homes.

Make a mosaic fish

Many Roman buildings were decorated with mosaics – pictures or patterns made up of lots of tiny squares of pottery or stone pressed into wet plaster. In this project, you can make a mosaic picture using small squares of coloured paper glued on to a thick sheet of card.

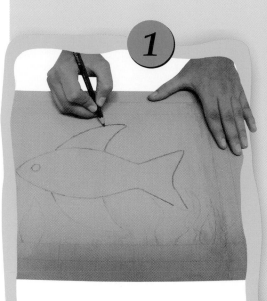

Lightly sketch your design on to the sheet of cardboard.

Roman mosaics

To make a mosaic, the Romans first traced a picture or pattern on to a wall or floor. Plaster was then spread on to the surface a small area at a time. The mosaic tiles (called tesserae) were pressed into the wet plaster in neat, evenly spaced rows. The finished mosaic was covered with plaster, to fill in the gaps between the tiles, then the tiles were polished to make them shine.

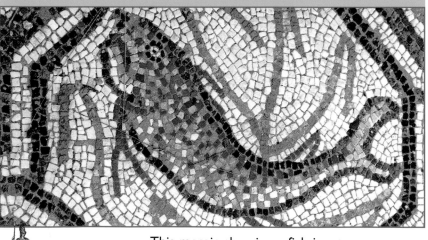

▲ This mosaic showing a fish is made up of thousands of tiny tiles.

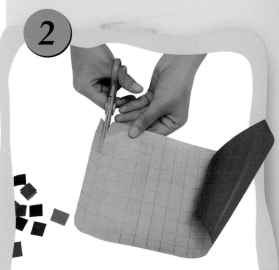

With a ruler, draw rows of squares each measuring 1.5 x 1.5cm on the back of sheets of coloured paper, then cut them out. You will need to cut some squares into smaller pieces to fit any odd-shaped gaps in your design.

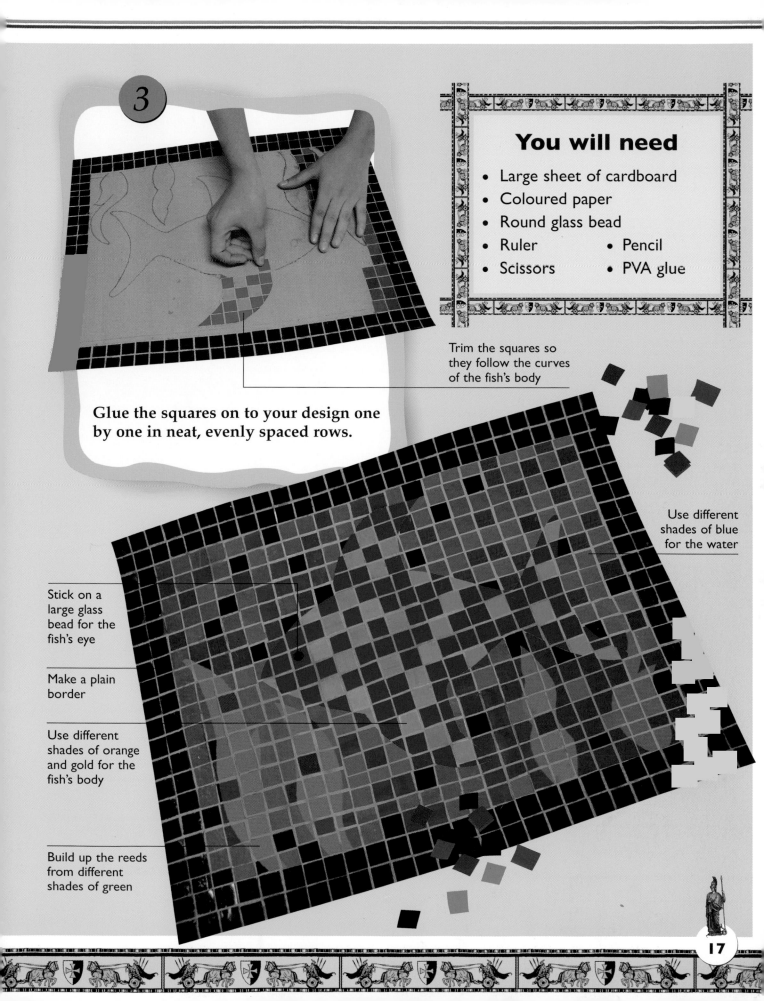

3

Trim the squares so they follow the curves of the fish's body

Glue the squares on to your design one by one in neat, evenly spaced rows.

Use different shades of blue for the water

Stick on a large glass bead for the fish's eye

Make a plain border

Use different shades of orange and gold for the fish's body

Build up the reeds from different shades of green

Friends and families

Romans relied on their friends and families. It was most unusual for a man or woman to live or work alone. A Roman family included everyone in the household, from the father, who was the paterfamilias (head), to children, old people and slaves.

A family duty

Roman men and women married young, usually in their teens. Marriages were often arranged by families. A Roman husband had to provide for all his family, and had the power of life and death over them. A Roman wife's main duty was to have a son and heir for her husband, and to manage the household. The Romans liked children but, in poor families, too many babies were a burden. Unwanted girls were left out of doors on rubbish heaps, to be adopted or die.

▲ Roman laws gave men power over the women in their families, but Roman women lived busy lives. Some rich women, like the girl in this wall-painting, learned to read and write.

▲ This mosaic dating from the 2nd century AD shows slaves and servants preparing for a feast.

Helping out

Many poor families worked together, in city shops and craft workshops or on farms. Rich families liked to make powerful friends, who could help them in business or politics. The rich also paid 'clients' (poor friends) to help them.

A nineteenth-century painting showing Roman ▲ guests reclining (leaning) side by side at a meal. Slaves bring them food and wine, while musicians entertain with songs and music.

Guests recline on couches, while the food and wine are served on a table in the centre

Guests use bread to scoop up their food or eat with their fingers

Having a meal

Eating together Sharing a meal with family and friends was a favourite Roman pastime. A meal was a chance to talk, relax, share news and views and, perhaps, enjoy music and poetry together.

Small meals Poor peoples' food was simple: bread, beans, porridge, onions and sour wine. Most houses did not have kitchens, so poor families bought take-away food from market stalls and bars.

Fine dining Rich people could afford elaborate dishes, especially at dinner time (late afternoon). They ate meat, fish, cheese, honey, fruit and fresh vegetables, cooked with herbs and spices, or flavoured with garum — fish sauce.

Top entertainers Star chefs were hired to cook for rich people's parties, where guests ate stretched out on couches. Favourite poets, singers and dancers performed to entertain guests. These dinner parties could last for many hours.

Play knucklebones

Knucklebones was a game played with the ankle bones of sheep. It was very popular in Ancient Greece and also played by adults and children in Ancient Rome. This project shows you how to make a set of knucklebones out of modelling clay, and gives you some rules so you can play the game.

Growing up

Roman parents and children enjoyed playing different kinds of games – especially at Saturnalia, the winter festival when everyone had fun. But Romans also valued hard work, for adults and youngsters. Boys from rich families went to school, or studied with private tutors, while boys from poor families worked with their fathers. They learned skills that would help them earn a living when they were around 7 years old.

A young boy playing ▶
knucklebones. Each bone had four long sides and two knobbly ends. When thrown, the bones landed on one of their long sides, each of which was given a value.

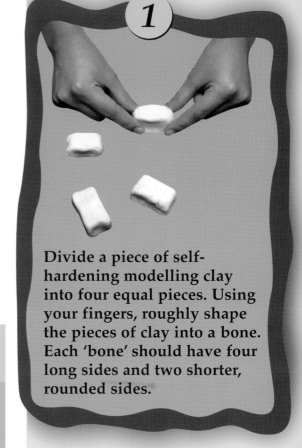

1

Divide a piece of self-hardening modelling clay into four equal pieces. Using your fingers, roughly shape the pieces of clay into a bone. Each 'bone' should have four long sides and two shorter, rounded sides.

Take turns to throw the bones – and throw all four bones at once.

If you throw a Venus (each bone shows a different score) you win the game!

2

When dry and hard, paint the clay 'bones' in a bright colour. Number each long side of each bone: 1, 3, 4 and 6. Use a contrasting colour for the numbers so they are easy to see.

The four long sides do not need to be smooth. The actual bones used in a game of knucklebones had four different sides: flat, concave (curving in), convex (curving out) and sinuous (curving in and out)

If you like, you can number the sides in Roman numerals – I for 1, III for 3, IV for 4 and VI for 6

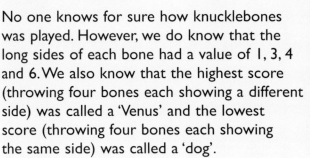

How to play

No one knows for sure how knucklebones was played. However, we do know that the long sides of each bone had a value of 1, 3, 4 and 6. We also know that the highest score (throwing four bones each showing a different side) was called a 'Venus' and the lowest score (throwing four bones each showing the same side) was called a 'dog'.

Here are some rules so you can play a game of knucklebones with a friend:

1. **Take turns to throw the set of four knucklebones on the floor.**

2. **Count up the number of points from each throw according to which sides land face up.**

3. **If a player throws a 'dog' (four of the same number), they lose the game. If a player throws a 'Venus' (each bone with a different number), they win the game.**

4. **The first player to reach an agreed number of points wins.**

Use a pen and paper to keep the scores.

You will need

- Self-hardening modelling clay
- Poster paint
- Metallic paint (optional)
- Paintbrush

Guardian gods

Religion played an important part in the lives of the Roman people. In public, they worshipped the gods and goddesses who protected Rome, and honoured the spirits of dead emperors. In private, they prayed to spirits that guarded their homes, or lived in rivers, mountains and forests.

Religious practices and superstitions

Men, women and children left offerings to the gods at temples. They slept in temples overnight, hoping to be healed, or left messages asking the gods to curse their enemies.

At home, families gave a share of their food to the Lares (household gods) and Penates (gods of the store-cupboard). Roman people also feared ghosts, wore lucky charms, consulted witches (though this was against the law) and were superstitious. It was bad luck to sneeze – but seeing a snake was good luck!

Statue of a Lar (one of the ▶ Roman household gods) who guarded the home and all the people who lived in it.

Worshipper carries parchment scroll, with the words of special prayers

Roman priests made public, ▲ open-air sacrifices of animals, and offered food and wine to please the gods, and ask for their help and guidance. They studied the flight of birds, or the insides of dead beasts, hoping to foresee the future.

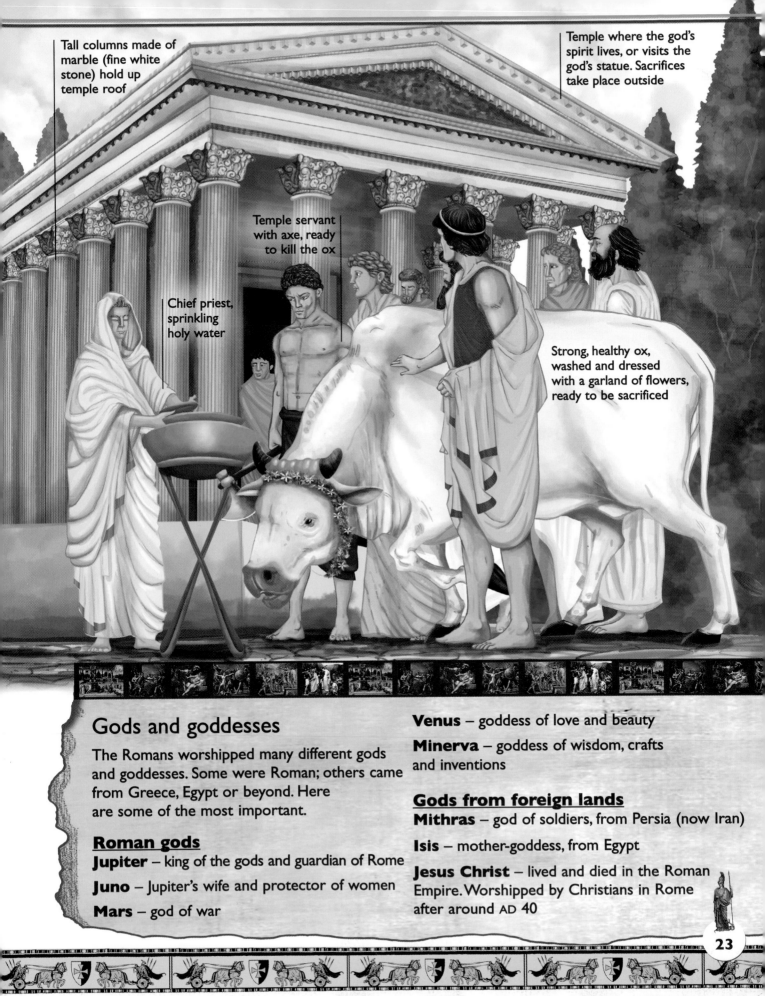

Tall columns made of marble (fine white stone) hold up temple roof

Temple where the god's spirit lives, or visits the god's statue. Sacrifices take place outside

Temple servant with axe, ready to kill the ox

Chief priest, sprinkling holy water

Strong, healthy ox, washed and dressed with a garland of flowers, ready to be sacrificed

Gods and goddesses

The Romans worshipped many different gods and goddesses. Some were Roman; others came from Greece, Egypt or beyond. Here are some of the most important.

Roman gods

Jupiter – king of the gods and guardian of Rome

Juno – Jupiter's wife and protector of women

Mars – god of war

Venus – goddess of love and beauty

Minerva – goddess of wisdom, crafts and inventions

Gods from foreign lands

Mithras – god of soldiers, from Persia (now Iran)

Isis – mother-goddess, from Egypt

Jesus Christ – lived and died in the Roman Empire. Worshipped by Christians in Rome after around AD 40

Make a bulla and lucky charms

Roman children wore a bulla around their necks. The bulla could be a small leather pouch or a golden locket, hung on a cord or chain. Each bulla contained an amulet or charm, to keep the wearer safe. Boys usually wore a bulla until they were about 16 years old. Girls wore them until they married.

Superstitions

Romans believed that the gods sent them good luck or bad luck, happiness and tragedy. So parents protected each child with a bulla and looked out for signs from the gods to show what the future might hold. Bees brought happiness and riches; snakes brought good luck. Signs of misfortune were a sneeze, hearing an owl hoot at night or falling over out of doors.

The Romans also believed that their dead ancestors had the power to help or harm them. Parents and children visited ancestors' tombs on holy days to show respect and make offerings of food and drink to their spirits.

This gold bulla, shaped liked a ▶ little bag, was made for a child from a very rich Roman family to wear.

Bulla

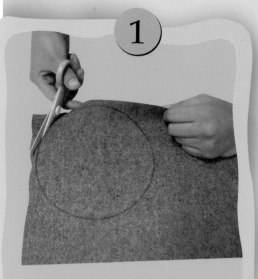

Cut out a circle of fabric measuring 10–15cm in diameter. Draw around a dish or saucer to get an even shape.

Lucky charms

Lucky snake

Tiny sword

Laurel wreath

Make some tiny amulets out of self-hardening modelling clay. You could model some simple peg-shaped figures, a tiny sword, a laurel wreath or an animal.

2

Fold the fabric over and ask an adult to help you snip a small slit just in from the edge. Do this at regular intervals all around the circle.

3

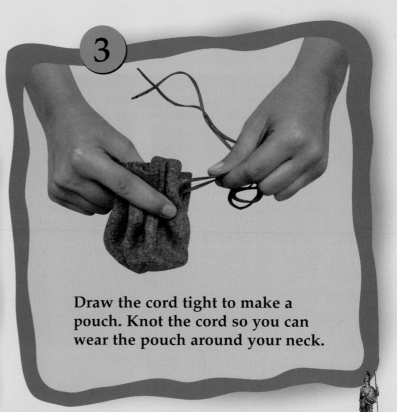

Thread a length of cord, about 70cm long, in and out of the slits.

You will need

Bulla:
- Fabric, such as thin leather or felt
- Dish or saucer
- Leather cord • Scissors

Lucky charms:
- Self-hardening modelling clay
- Poster paints • Paintbrushes

2

When the clay is hard and dry, paint your lucky charms with poster paints. Pop the charms in your bulla when the paint is dry.

3

Draw the cord tight to make a pouch. Knot the cord so you can wear the pouch around your neck.

Sports and games

Strict rules banned Romans from working on religious festival days. So they enjoyed their time off by watching sports, playing games, listening to music or going the theatre.

Two or four horses pull each chariot. Four-horse chariots are faster

Young Roman women athletes and dancers in training. One (top left) ▲ carries dumbbells (weights to tone and strengthen muscles); three (top and bottom, right) are practising throwing balls.

Most popular sports

Favourite Roman spectator sports included chariot racing, and fights between gladiators, criminals or animals. Vast crowds flocked to watch these events, attracted by the skill, speed, bloodthirstiness and danger. Top charioteers and gladiators often died young, but their lives were full of glamour and glory. They attracted rich sponsors, devoted fans and beautiful girlfriends – just like footballers today.

▲ A gladiator comes face to face with a lion in a Roman wild beast show. Lions and other large or fierce animals were specially shipped from Africa to Rome to be killed.

Tall columns, called metae, mark the turning point at each end of the track

Most charioteers were originally slaves. If they were successful they might be able to buy their freedom

Spectators cheer their teams. There are seats for 250,000 to watch each race

▼ In Rome, chariot races were held at a stadium called the Circus Maximus. Teams raced anticlockwise round a long, oval track. A race lasted for seven circuits, a distance of 8km.

Horses for racing were specially bred. The best came from Spain

Accidents often happen when chariots crash or overturn

Chariots are lightweight, and built for speed, but are often richly decorated

Music, dance and theatre

Music and dance accompanied most important stages in each Roman's life, especially their wedding and their funeral. Music was also part of solemn religious ceremonies.

Musical instruments The most popular instruments were flutes, panpipes, cymbals and lyres. On the battlefield, Roman soldiers sent signals by blowing trumpets and horns.

Poetry and music Poets often sang their works to musical accompaniment. Music at theatres helped to add excitement to performances, or create a special mood. The chorus (a group of backing actors) danced and sang, keeping in time and tune.

On stage Actors in Roman theatres wore wigs, masks and heavy costumes. Their masks showed just a few expressions, mostly happy or sad. The masks were designed to be seen and understood even by spectators right at the back of the theatre.

Make gladiator weapons

There were many different kinds of gladiators. A Retiarius (net-fighter) was armed with a net to trap his opponent and a three-pointed spear to kill him. He had little protection; only his spear-arm was covered with armour. A Secutor (pursuer) moved more slowly, weighed down by a helmet, leg-guards, heavy sword and maybe a shield. A Velitis (skirmisher) had no armour at all. He fought in a team of five, throwing javelins at an enemy team. Here is how to make a round gladiator shield and a sword.

Gladiator sword

1

Cut out two identical pieces of thick card, in the shape of a sword blade, about 45cm long. Glue the pieces together, then cover them in silver foil.

Forced to fight

Most gladiators were either criminals being punished, or prisoners captured in war. They were condemned to fight and die in a very horrible way. Some were sent to gladiator schools so they could learn to fight more skilfully and provide more entertainment for the crowds in their short, bloody appearance in the arena.

This mosaic shows ▶ two gladiators in deadly combat. The man on the left has lost — or thrown away — his shield, but is moving in close to try to stab his opponent.

Shield

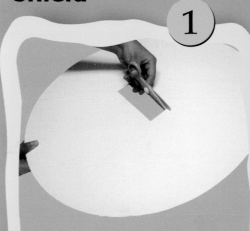

1

Cut two identical circles out of card about 50–60cm in diameter. Ask an adult to help you cut a rectangular slot measuring 14 x 3cm in the middle of one circle.

2

Cut out a rectangle of card measuring 15 x 10cm. Make a slit in the centre of the card, a little wider than the sword blade.

3

Slide the card on to the blade, fold it down and glue it about 7cm from the top, to make the sword's hilt.

Wrap coloured tape around the sword handle and hilt, to keep the hilt in place

2

Cut a long strip of card 28cm long and 2.50–2.75cm wide. Cover the strip in brown tape. Push the card into the slot to make a handle, firmly taping down the ends.

You will need

- Thick card
- Poster paints
- Coloured tape
- Paintbrush
- Gold or bronze metallic paint
- Silver foil
- Scissors
- PVA glue
- Sticky tape

Tape a card cone, painted bronze or gold, to the centre of your shield

Paint the shield with poster paints in colours of your choice

Make studs out of card circles painted in bronze or gold metallic paint

3

Glue the two circles together, so the stuck down ends of the handle are on the inside, then decorate the front of the shield.

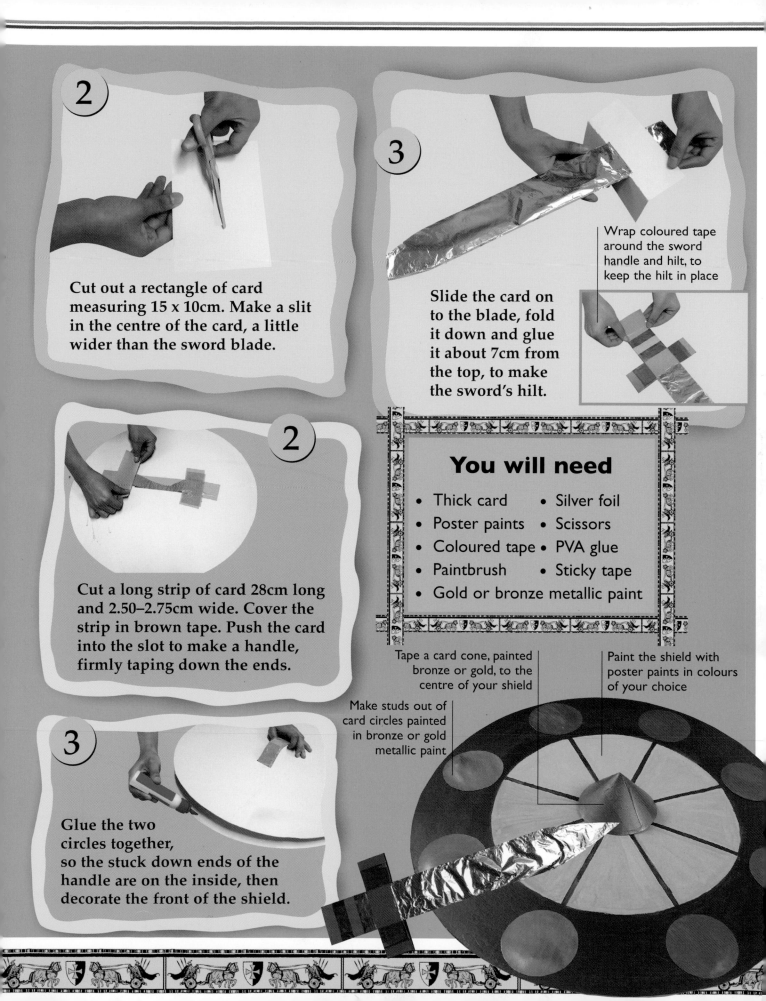

Timeline

753 BC According to legend, King Romulus founds Rome.

509 BC Last Roman king, Tarquin the Proud, is overthrown.

509 BC Rome becomes a republic.

390 BC Celtic warriors attack Rome.

334–264 BC Roman armies win control of all Italy.

312 BC Romans start many big building projects, including the Via Appia, the first main road leading out of Rome.

264–146 BC Three wars between Rome and the city of Carthage in North Africa, for control of the Mediterranean Sea.

73 BC Slave-leader Spartacus leads a revolt against Rome slave owners.

58–51 BC Julius Caesar conquers Gaul and invades Britain.

44 BC Julius Caesar is murdered.

27 BC Augustus becomes first emperor of Rome.

AD 43 Romans conquer Britain.

AD 60-61 Boudicca, queen of a Celtic tribe, the Iceni, leads a rebellion against Rome.

AD 64 Great Fire destroys a large part of Rome. Emperor Nero blames the Christians.

AD 79 Volcano Vesuvius erupts and buries the town of Pompeii, south of Rome, in lava.

AD 117 Reign of emperor Hadrian begins. Roman Empire at its peak.

AD 212 All inhabitants of the Roman Empire become Roman citizens.

AD 313 Christians are allowed religious freedom in the Roman Empire.

AD 330 Emperor Constantine founds a new eastern capital city, Constantinople (now Istanbul).

AD 395 Roman Empire is divided into eastern and western halves.

AD 410 Invaders attack the city of Rome. Roman power weakens.

AD 476 The last emperor flees Rome. Roman power collapses in Western Europe. The eastern half of the Roman Empire survives, as a new state, Byzantium.

Glossary

Aqueduct Raised channel to carry water, usually to a big city.

Chorus Group of actors who stood on stage, singing, dancing and commenting on the actions of other characters in a play.

Clients Poor people who accepted food or money from a rich family in return for helping and supporting them.

Consuls Elected judges who ruled Rome when it was a republic.

Emperor Sole, male ruler of an empire.

Forum Central meeting place in a Roman city.

Garum Strong-tasting, salty sauce made from rotten fish.

Insula (plural insulae) Apartment blocks in Roman towns and cities. The name means 'islands', because each block was separate from the rest of the community.

Lares Household gods who guard the people living in a home.

Lyre Musical instrument like a small harp.

Panpipes Musical instrument made of several short pipes linked together.

Paterfamilias Father of a family; head of each Roman household.

Patricians Rich, noble families in Rome.

Penates Household gods of food and security. Said to live in each family's store-cupboard.

Plebeians Poor, ordinary Roman people.

Republic A state or nation in which the people or their elected representatives hold supreme power.

Senate Committee of rich noblemen who elected the Consuls and advised the government of Rome.

Senator Member of the Senate; Roman politician.

Spectator sports Sports that are watched by large crowds of people.

Tyrant Powerful, cruel, unjust ruler.

Villa Country house, which was usually the centre of a large farm estate.

Index

Webfinder

http://www.roman-empire.net/index.html
A vast interactive site covering all aspects of the Roman Empire.

http://members.aol.com/Donnclass/Romelife.html
http://www.bbc.co.uk/schools/romans/
Both these sites focus on Roman life, aimed at children.

http://www.kidskonnect.com/content/view/262/27/
Provides links to sites about Rome for children.

MAKING HISTORY

SERIES CONTENTS

EGYPT

River kingdom • Pharaohs and priests • Dress like an Egyptian • On the banks of the Nile
Make a shaduf • Living in a town • Make Egyptian jewellery • Friends and family • Play 'Snake'
Writing, counting and discovering • Make a lucky pendant • Everlasting life
Make a mummy mask • Timeline • Glossary
Index and Webfinder

ROME

What do we know about the Romans? • City and people • Dress like a Roman • Army and empire
Make a Roman standard • Brilliant builders • Make a mosaic fish • Friends and families
Play knucklebones • Guardian gods • Make a bulla and lucky charms • Sports and games
Make gladiator weapons • Timeline • Glossary • Index and Webfinder

PIRATES

World of piracy • Caribbean buccaneers • Dress like a pirate • Corsairs and privateers
Make a treasure chest • Pirate ships • Make a pirate flag • Life on board • Make a pirate's fruit salad
Attack at sea • Make a pirate's dagger • Treasure! • Make a treasure map and case
Timeline • Glossary • Index and Webfinder

KNIGHTS

Knights and chivalry • Becoming a knight • Dress like a knight • Clothing and armour
Make a knight's helmet • Weapons • Make a sword and shield • Castles
Play Fox and Geese • Tournaments • Make some pennants • Knightly orders
Make a jewelled chalice • Timeline • Glossary • Index and Webfinder

VICTORIANS

Who were the Victorians? • Queen and country • Make a top hat • Workshop of the world
Make a loom • How to weave • Rich lives, poor lives • Scrapbooking • Fun and games
Victorian Christmas; make some decorations • New inventions, new discoveries • Make a zoetrope
The British Empire • Timeline • Glossary • Index and Webfinder

WORLD WAR TWO

The world at war • Outbreak of war • Food rationing game • War in the skies
Making model planes • The Home Front • Make do and mend (How to make a rag doll)
The war at sea • Propaganda • Dig For Victory • Spies and secret services in World War Two
Spies and spying in World War Two • The end of the war • Victory
Glossary • Index and Webfinder